HAUNTED OR HOAX?

HAUNTED TOWNS AND VILLAGES

VIC KOVACS

CRABTREE
PUBLISHING COMPANY
WWW.CRABTREEBOOKS.COM

HAUNTED OR HOAX?

Author: Vic Kovacs

Editors: Janice Dyer, Marcia Abramson, Petrice Custance

Photo research: Melissa McClellan

Cover/interior design: T.J. Choleva

Proofreader: Lorna Notsch

Production coordinator and prepress technician: Tammy McGarr

Print coordinator: Katherine Berti

Consultant: Susan Demeter-St. Clair
Paranormal Studies & Inquiry

Written and produced for Crabtree Publishing by BlueAppleWorks Inc.

Photographs & Illustrations

Cover illustration: T.J Choleva (background image: Kochneva Tetyana/Shutterstock; front image: Captblack76/Shutterstock;
Title page illustration: Joshua Avramson (front image: MaxShutter/Shutterstock;
Shutterstock.com: © Login (page backgrounds); © Fer Gregory (p. 4); © Venus Kaewyoo (p. 5, 19 middle); © andreiuc88 (p. 5 sidebar); © Basileus (p. 9, 23 sidebar); © Daniel Korzeniewski (p. 10 top right); © Andrey_Kuzmin (p. 11, 27 middle); © Felix Mizioznikov (p. 11 top right, 11 bottom); © Imagine Photographer (p. 11, 13, 27 sidebar); © Ensuper (p. 13, 29 middle); © jannoon028 (p. 14–15 bottom); © Joseph Becker (p. 15, 23 middle); © Tony Craddock/Shutterstock.com (p. 15 top right); © TaTum2003 (p. 15 sidebar); © WAYHOME studio (p. 18 bottom left); © Aleksey Stemmer (p. 19 sidebar); © George Burba (p. 20 top right); © vagabond54 (p. 20 middle right); © Nejron Photo (p. 20 bottom right); © kaetana (p. 24 top right); © Kanuman (p. 25 top right); © Lev Kropotov (p. 25 middle); © Ozerov Alexander (p. 25 sidebar); © suren1919 (p. 26 top right); © Zhao jian kang/Shutterstock.com (p. 26 middle right); © Pommy.Anyani/Shutterstock.com (p. 26 bottom right); © Daniel Prudek (p. 27 top right); © d13 (p. 28 top right); © Nomad_Soul (p. 29 sidebar)
Creative Commons: Ebyabe (p. 13 top right); Daniel Mayer (p. 14 top right); Graham Ellis (p. 18 top right); Pradeep717 (p. 22–23 bottom); Joshua Avramson p. 6 (background image Blackdoll/Creative Commons); p. 9; p. 10 bottom (background image Kenneth Keifer/Shutterstock.com); p. 17 (front image Master1305/Shutterstock.com); p. 21 (front image Yevhen Rehulian/Shutterstock.com);p. 17 (front image Olesya Kozhevnikova/Shutterstock.com; background image Alexander Mazurkevich/Shutterstock.com); T.J Choleva p. 7 (background image Mcpikemansioncrew/Creative Commons); p. 8; p. 12 (background image Ebyabe/Creative Commons); p. 18 (background image nz_willowherb/Creative Commons); p. 28 bottom (front image Joerg Steber/Shutterstock.com)
Carlyn Iverson p. 15; 27

Library and Archives Canada Cataloguing in Publication

Kovacs, Vic, author
    Haunted towns and villages / Vic Kovacs.

(Haunted or hoax?)
Includes index.
Issued in print and electronic formats.
ISBN 978-0-7787-4631-7 (hardcover).--
ISBN 978-0-7787-4642-3 (softcover).--
ISBN 978-1-4271-2055-7 (HTML)

    1. Haunted places--Juvenile literature. 2. Cities and towns--
Juvenile literature. 3. Villages--Juvenile literature. 4. Ghosts--Juvenile
literature. I. Title.

BF1461.K68 2018   j133.1'22   C2017-907788-0
                                    C2017-907789-9

Library of Congress Cataloging-in-Publication Data

CIP available at the Library of Congress

Crabtree Publishing Company

www.crabtreebooks.com   1-800-387-7650

Printed in the U.S.A./032018/BG20180202

Published in Canada
Crabtree Publishing
616 Welland Ave.
St. Catharines, Ontario
L2M 5V6

Published in the United States
Crabtree Publishing
PMB 59051
350 Fifth Avenue, 59th Floor
New York, New York 10118

Published in the United Kingdom
Crabtree Publishing
Maritime House
Basin Road North, Hove
BN41 1WR

Published in Australia
Crabtree Publishing
3 Charles Street
Coburg North
VIC, 3058

CONTENTS

PARANORMAL INVESTIGATIONS

People have been telling ghost stories for centuries. Some ghost stories are told to entertain. Others are told as a way to warn people about certain places or behaviors. And some are told just to terrify people! Most ghost stories are told as if they are true. Usually this is because saying a ghostly encounter really happened makes it that much spookier. But other times, the teller really believes the story is true. It's important to think about whether the ghost stories you hear are true or if there could be another explanation. If you look at them carefully and **critically**, you can usually figure it out. And who knows? Maybe one day you'll come across a ghost story that is real!

DID YOU KNOW?

In England, telling ghost stories used to be a Christmas tradition! Many say that the author M.R. James invented the modern ghost story. He wrote most of his stories to tell to his friends around the fire on Christmas Eve.

Believers and Skeptics

Some people work hard trying to figure out if ghostly tales are true. These people are called **paranormal** investigators. These investigators have a number of different skills. They research local history. They talk to people to gather first-hand witness reports. Then they must be brave enough to go to locations where ghosts are reported and look for **evidence** of the **supernatural**. They also use a number of different tools to help in their work.

There are also people who aren't convinced ghosts exist. They're called **skeptics**. Skeptics look at the supernatural from every angle. They try to see if there's a way to explain an event without blaming ghosts. Maybe a spooky scream was just a bird call. Maybe a flickering light was damaged wiring. While you read the stories in this book, see if you can come up with explanations for the things that happen that don't involve the paranormal.

Some ghosts are said to take the form of a person. Others are reported as a swirl of mist, a sound, or even a feeling.

TOOLS OF THE TRADE

Early ghost hunters had only simple tools like candles and mirrors. Today, there are many high-tech devices that can be used to track ghosts. Here are three of the main ones:

EMF Meter: EMF stands for **electromagnetic field**. This device can detect and measure the energy being produced by objects. Some ghost hunters believe that abnormal EMF readings mean that a ghost is near. Skeptics believe the readings are caused by wiring or other electrically charged objects in the area.

Digital Voice Recorder: This device can record notes and interviews, as well as electronic voice **phenomena**, or EVP. Ghost hunters believe it's possible to record the voices of ghosts and play them back.

Camera: A camera, digital or film, is an invaluable ghost-hunting tool. Cameras that can take photos in low light, or that have **night vision**, are the most helpful for tracking ghosts. Some investigators believe cameras can pick up on things that would normally be invisible to the human eye.

AMERICA'S MOST HAUNTED SMALL TOWN

Almost every town in America claims to have at least one haunted house or building. Alton, Illinois, however, claims to have several. So many ghosts have been reported that some people consider Alton the most haunted small town in America.

Innocent Beginnings

The most famous and possibly haunted building in Alton is the McPike Mansion. It was built in 1869 for Henry McPike and his family. He was a **horticulturist** who grew award-winning grapes. He also was mayor of Alton for a time. After his death, new owner Paul Laichinger turned the home into a boarding house. He died in 1945, and the house fell into disrepair.

Boarders at McPike Mansion (at right) said they heard children playing when no kids were there. After the home became vacant, people said they saw ghostly faces peering out from the broken windows.

The Ghosts Appear

In 1994, Sharyn and George Luedke bought the mansion. They hoped to restore it and open a bed and breakfast. Soon after, Sharyn was digging in the front garden. She says she looked up and saw a man in old-fashioned clothes staring at her through a window. Later, she came upon a picture of Paul Laichinger. Not only did the man she had seen look just like him, he was wearing the exact same clothes!

There are other ghostly stories surrounding the McPike Mansion. Visitors have reported seeing the figure of a woman, thought to be the ghost of a former servant named Sarah. The house is also famous for photos that show strange, glowing **orbs**. A number of people say they have even taken videos showing these orbs.

Some visitors say they smell the lilac perfume of the ghost Sarah in the attic of the mansion. Sharyn Luedke says she has felt Sarah hug her.

Haunted Mansion

Alton was a busy stop on the **Underground Railroad**, the network that helped move escaped slaves to freedom in the 1800s. One important stop along the railroad was the Nathaniel Hanson Mansion. Hanson was an **abolitionist**, someone who strongly believed that all slaves should be free. He built his house to help this cause. The builders carved tunnels beneath the house where people could hide. The house also had specially built lanterns to signal whether it was safe for people to make their way to the mansion. In the early 1900s, the house was converted into a **sanatorium** for people with **tuberculosis**. It was renamed the Enos Sanatorium. At that time, there was no cure for tuberculosis. Because of this, many people died within its walls.

Some people say they hear the ghosts of patients coughing at the sanatorium. Others report seeing the ghost of a slave who died while hiding there.

Ghosts Everywhere!

More recently, the building was converted into an impressive apartment building. Residents have reported a number of strange events. Toilets flush when there's nobody in the bathroom. Footsteps echo down empty hallways. Some people have even heard screams.

These are just some of the places in Alton that people say are haunted by ghosts or spirits. There is also the First Unitarian Church. Another is an old prison that held Confederate soldiers during the Civil War. Some even say that an old cracker factory is haunted!

HAUNTED RAILROAD

African Americans used the Underground Railroad to escape slavery in the southern states in the 1800s. They traveled to northern states or to Canada using a secret network of safe houses.

The people running the network used railroad terms to hide what they were doing. For example, they called escaped slaves "passengers," "cargo," "packages," or "freight." They called the safe houses "stations" or "depots." The owners identified their safe houses by lighting candles in the windows or placing lanterns outside.

The safe houses had secret rooms in the attics and basements. The runaways hid in these rooms to escape slave catchers and bounty hunters. Tragically, some escaped slaves died in these hiding places from starvation, injuries, or disease. Some say the safe houses are now haunted by the restless spirits of the dead.

LOOK AT THE EVIDENCE

When deciding if a place is really haunted, you have to look at the evidence. Evidence might take the form of photos, videos, tape recordings, eyewitness accounts, and more. Let's look at some of the evidence in the McPike Mansion case.

One of the main eyewitness accounts of the McPike hauntings comes from one of the house's owners. That same owner runs a business giving ghost tours of the building. Is it possible that she may have claimed to see a ghost to encourage visitors to the area? Are you convinced by the evidence?

GHOSTS OF THE ANCIENT CITY

St. Augustine, in northeastern Florida, was settled by the Spanish in 1565, long before the Pilgrims arrived at Plymouth Rock in 1620. St. Augustine is the oldest European settlement in the United States that has been occupied since its founding. It has earned the nickname of "the Ancient City."

With such a long history, it shouldn't be surprising that a few residents may have decided to stick around St. Augustine— even after they've died! Many ghosts have been reported in the town. Some paranormal researchers consider the Ancient City to be one of the most haunted towns in the United States.

Many people visit St. Augustine each year to see the historic sites. Ghost tours at night are part of the fun.

Several of St. Augustine's many ghost stories are about Delores, the Woman in White. Her name means "sorrows" in Spanish.

Wandering Delores

One of the oldest buildings in St. Augustine is the Castillo de San Marcos, also called the Old Fort. The original structure was finished in 1695, but it has since seen much more construction. The building played a role in a number of wars and battles over the years. It's now thought to be home to a number of spirits. The most famous of these is Delores Marti. Delores was the wife of the commander of the fort. He suspected that she was spending too much time with one of his soldiers. He even thought he smelled her perfume on the soldier. Shortly after, both Delores and the soldier disappeared. The soldier was never seen again. But it's said Delores still wanders the fort's grounds in a beautiful white dress.

So many ghosts have been reported at the Old Fort that it has been featured on Ghost Adventures, Ghost Hunters, Monumental Mysteries, *and other TV shows. The ghosts are said to include pirates and soldiers.*

ST. AUGUSTINE LIGHTHOUSE

The St. Augustine Lighthouse is often considered the most haunted place in the entire city. A number of tragedies have taken place there over the years. A lighthouse keeper named Joseph Andreu fell to his death in 1859 while painting the lighthouse. While a new lighthouse was being built in 1873, three young girls were drowned after being trapped in a supply cart. Visitors report hearing girls laugh and seeing their ghosts around the grounds. One local tour guide said a ghost grabbed his ankle! Despite its spooky reputation, the lighthouse is still in operation today. But now it's mostly controlled by computers.

Ghost's Teeth

Another haunted site in St. Augustine is the Huguenot Cemetery. One of its best-known ghost stories is about a judge named John B. Stickney. In life, Stickney was loved by his fellow residents for offering them free legal advice if it was too expensive for them to afford. After his death and burial in the Huguenot Cemetery, the judge's family decided to move away from St. Augustine. They wanted his body to be moved to the graveyard in their new town. It is said that after Stickney's body was dug up, thieves stole the gold teeth right out of his mouth. Some people believe this theft upset his spirit. Today, visitors claim to have seen the judge's ghost wandering among the graves. Maybe he's searching for his lost teeth!

Some ghost hunters use specially trained dogs to track spirits that may be roaming, like the judge. Many people believe that dogs can sniff out ghosts with their super sensing abilities.

Ghost Hunters' Paradise

Other haunted buildings in St. Augustine include the Casablanca Inn. Some say the inn is home to the ghost of the former owner, who made extra money by working as a lookout for **bootleggers** during **Prohibition** from 1920 to 1933. She would signal the bootleggers that the coast was clear to bring their liquor ashore by waving a lantern. Some report seeing the ghost waving a lantern.

People say these ghosts still call the Ancient City home, and probably will for generations to come. Both new and experienced ghost hunters can find much to explore in St. Augustine.

MOANING GHOSTS OF THE OLD JAIL

The Old Jail is said to be one of the most haunted places in St. Augustine, and for good reason. The jail opened in 1891. Male and female criminals were kept there in horrible conditions. Many of them were executed, while others died from illnesses because of the living conditions.

The ghosts that haunt the Old Jail are said to be the spirits of these dead people. Ghost hunters say they have heard voices, moaning, and shouting when visiting the jail. Others report hearing prisoners' chains clanging, along with footsteps. Some even say they were pushed or tripped by a ghost when visiting one of the women's cells. Ghosts have also been spotted in different parts of the jail. Some say one ghost is often seen in the kitchen area, while another seems to disappear into a wall.

LOOK AT THE EVIDENCE

When visiting a "haunted" location, people often learn about its history. Some experts think that knowing this information might make people more likely to blame things on ghosts. For example, say you're at the St. Augustine Lighthouse on a tour. You learn that the area may be haunted, and you hear the story about the little girls who drowned. Suddenly, you hear a loud high-pitched sound. Your brain immediately connects the sound to the story you just heard. You're convinced you heard the little girls laughing. But is that the only explanation? Could the sound be something as simple as a bird crying out? What do you think?

The term "ghost town" can mean different things. It can refer to a town that is thought to be home to spooks, **specters,** and **apparitions**. This could describe pretty much every town mentioned in this book. A more common definition of ghost town is a town that has been abandoned by all its living residents. The town of Bodie, California, is a ghost town in every sense of the phrase.

In its heyday, Bodie had about 65 saloons similar to the one shown above. Gamblers and gunslingers would gather in them.

Abandoned by the Living

Bodie was originally a small mining camp. Then a major gold deposit was found nearby in 1876. Almost overnight, Bodie was transformed into a gold rush boom town. Thousands of people traveled there hoping to find their fortune. Then gold was discovered in other areas. Many **prospectors** moved on. Bodie became a quieter mining town. However, the population kept getting smaller. Eventually, it was completely abandoned. Abandoned, at least, by the living.

Bad Luck Charms

Today, Bodie is preserved as a state park. The empty town is full of buildings that are still standing. Many of these buildings and homes are filled with items that people left behind when they abandoned the town. This creates an eerie feeling for many visitors. While there are a number of stories involving individual ghosts, the most famous paranormal event involves these forgotten items. It's said that anyone who attempts to remove any item from Bodie will be cursed with bad luck. People who have taken souvenirs from the town have reported money trouble, car wrecks, and other misfortunes. Some say the curse can be stopped by returning whatever item was taken. Because of this, park rangers at Bodie claim to receive many returned items in the mail every year. Sometimes these items even come with apology letters!

About 60 structures remain in Bannack. Like Bodie, it is now a state park that can be explored.

BANNACK, MONTANA

Bodie isn't the only ghost town that exists because of a gold rush. Bannack, Montana, was once a successful mining town. However, its last living residents left in the 1970s. Gold rush towns were known to be rough places, and Bannack was no exception. One story says that the local sheriff, Henry Plummer, was actually the leader of a gang of murderous bandits. He was hanged by people trying to protect the town. However, whether or not Plummer was actually responsible for any crime is a matter of some debate. His ghost is said to wander the abandoned town, hoping to clear his name.

THE MOST HAUNTED VILLAGE IN BRITAIN?

England is home to a number of ancient towns and villages. The village of Bramshott is known to have existed as far back as 1086. It is located on an old road halfway between London and the city of Portsmouth. It became a popular stopover for travelers making their way between the two cities. Because of this, it also became popular with a less respectable kind of person.

The Seven Thorns was a busy inn until trains and cars came along. It became a pub, but closed in the 1990s due to a fire.

Highwaymen from Hell

Highwaymen were criminals who robbed travelers. They would wait by the side of the road. When a person or stagecoach passed by, the highwaymen would ride up and demand money and valuables. Even if the travelers did everything a highwayman demanded, there was no guarantee they would escape with their life.

Seventeen Ghosts of Bramshott

The Bramshott Inn, known as the Seven Thorns, became a well-known hangout for highwaymen and other rough characters. It was used as a meet-up and planning spot for plenty of unpleasant people. Because of the visitors it attracted, it was a very dangerous place. It's said that many of the Bramshott ghosts exist because of deaths and murders that happened there. One boy was killed by highwaymen while trying to do his job serving ale at the inn. Another was killed by a gang of highwaymen while looking after their horses.

These are just a few of the 17 ghosts that are said to haunt the houses and alleys of Bramshott. No wonder it is often called England's most haunted village!

Many people say they have seen the ghost of a highwayman named Jack on the road or at the Anchor Hotel in Bramshott where he was shot to death.

LADY of LAWERS

Loch is an old **Gaelic** word that means a lake or a sea inlet. Loch Tay is located in Scotland. The old abandoned village of Lawers is on its north shore. In the 1600s, this village was home to the Lady of Lawers. She was known in the area as a soothsayer, or someone who could see the future.

People have come to Loch Tay since ancient times for its good fishing, especially for salmon.

Some say the Lady of Lawers roams near the ruined church because she was buried there.

Doomed Church Roof

One day, while the village church was being built, the lady was heard to say that the stones for the roof would never be put in place. At first, people laughed, since the boat bringing the stones was already on its way. However, that night, a terrible storm swept over the loch, and the boat sank. After that, people started believing the things the Lady of Lawers had to say.

Cursed Tree

The Lady of Lawers also planted a beautiful ash tree beside the church. She warned that if anyone harmed the tree, evil would come to them. Many years later, a local farmer decided to cut the tree down, even though he knew the warning. Soon after, the farmer was **gored** to death by one of his bulls. A friend who had helped him cut the tree down went completely insane. Even the horse that hauled the tree away from the church dropped dead. Visitors to the village claim to have seen a ghostly woman walking amid its ruins. Many believe it to be the ghost of the Lady of Lawers.

LADY OF LAWERS PROPHECIES

The Lady of Lawers made a number of predictions that seem to have come true. For example, she said "fire coaches" would be seen in the area. In the 1800s, a railway line was built where she predicted. She also said that the area around Lawers would see "a mill on every stream and a plough in every field." In fact, by the end of the 1700s, 14 mills and 200 plows were being used in the area to farm and process flax.

LOOK AT THE EVIDENCE

Since the Lady of Lawers died, her legend has only grown. It's important to remember, though, that only some of her predictions seem to have been correct. Messages that predict what could happen in the future can be tricky things. These messages are often stated in a vague way and can mean different things. As a result, when something happens that seems close to what the prediction said was going to happen, people tend to say it came true. What do you think? Could the Lady of Lawers see into the future? Or did she just make some lucky guesses?

GHOSTS OF THE ANCIENT VIKING VILLAGE

L'Anse aux Meadows is a beautiful spot where the locals make their living by fishing. It is located on the northernmost tip of Newfoundland, Canada. In the 1960s, the only confirmed Viking settlement in North America was found there.

Long-gone Visitors

Vikings were tough, seafaring people from Scandinavia. They were known for conducting brutal raids all across Europe. **Archaeologists** believe their settlement in Newfoundland may have been home to as many as 130 people. At that time, the area was heavily forested. This made it perfect for boatbuilding, which was one of the major occupations of the Vikings. Although it's been about 1,000 years since these Nordic settlers lived in the area, locals claim that they left behind a ghostly reminder of their time there.

The Viking settlement has been recreated as a living history site.

No one knows why the Vikings left L'Anse aux Meadows. One possible reason was a lack of game to hunt. Another was fierce fighting with the Inuit peoples who already lived there. The Vikings ended up staying only about 10 years.

Vanishing Ship

One day in late summer, all the local fishermen were in a great mood. They had all had huge catches that day, and were quite happy about it. All but one fisherman went back home with the good news. He stayed behind to gut and clean his fish. While busy with his work, he heard a sound outside the shack he was in. It sounded like oars in the water. He went outside to investigate, but couldn't see a thing. Suddenly, he heard the sound of a huge horn, and a ship unlike anything he had ever seen came into view. The boat had one huge, square sail, and oarsmen on both sides, all rowing in unison. As quickly as it had come into view, it disappeared, right in front of his eyes.

Since then, it's said that same strange ship can be seen every 30 years, on the same day, August 15.

*Many of the local fishermen believe that seeing the ship is a good **omen**. They say it brings with it a good catch, just as the first time it was sighted.*

VANISHED OVERNIGHT

The village of Kuldhara, in India, has stood empty for a long time. It was abandoned in the early 1800s. No one is quite sure why. The village was home to a group known as the Paliwal Brahmin. They were respected in Indian society. They were talented businesspeople and skilled farmers who were able to grow crops in desert areas where no one else could.

According to one legend, all of the residents of Kuldhara abandoned the village in one night. They left their homes and all their belongings behind. It is said that the villagers cursed the town before they left. The curse said if anyone tried to settle in Kuldhara, they would be met with death and misfortune. Nobody saw the villagers leave, and nobody knows where they went.

Kuldhara was once a green oasis in the desert. Some historians believe that the people left because their water supplies were disappearing. A nearby riverbed is dry now, and the town is full of dried-up wells.

The Curse of Brahmin

Some say that a corrupt local official was one reason for the sudden flight from Kuldhara. This man, Salim Singh, had already set harsh taxes on the Paliwal Brahmin. One day, he fell in love with a young woman from the village. Some stories claim she was the daughter of the village chief. Singh demanded the woman's hand in marriage. If she was not delivered to him, he would raise taxes so high it would be impossible to live. So, one night, during the Hindu festival of Raksha Bandhan, all of the Paliwal Brahmin from Kuldhara and its surrounding villages came together and fled the village. More than 1,000 people disappeared overnight. As they left, it's said that the departing villagers placed the famous curse on their beloved village.

According to legend, it's the curse that makes the town so parched that no one can live there but spirits.

JATINGA BIRD SUICIDE

Imagine birds dropping dead from the sky for no reason. This is what seems to happen in the village of Jatinga in India. Visitors travel to the village just to see this unexplained event. It only takes place on moonless nights in September and October. Even more strangely, the birds only fall from the sky between 6:00 p.m. and 9:30 p.m., and they only fall in a specific part of the village. Locals call these events "bird suicides" to encourage tourists to come to the town. The authorities have even created a festival around the event.

Locals say these mass bird suicides have been happening every year for more than 100 years. So why does this happen? Scientists have offered a number of explanations. Some say the birds become confused from strong winds and fog. They fly toward the lights in the town, plunging to their death.

Although some birds do plummet to their death for no reason, in reality many villagers kill the birds because they believe they are spirits flying from the sky to terrorize them. Experts have started educating the villagers to try to stop the mass killings. They have succeeded in reducing bird deaths.

Frightening Ruins

Since then, Kuldhara has developed a reputation as a haunted village. Visitors have reported a number of different types of phenomena. Some have felt a ghostly tap on their shoulder. Others have seen shadows moving, unattached to people. Visitors also say they often hear footsteps and voices, with no clear sources.

The site became so well-known that it was even investigated by the Indian Paranormal Society. The group's leader claimed that one night, a child's handprint began appearing on every single car the group had driven to the village. The group members also said they observed temperature changes and located electromagnetic fields.

*Kuldhara today is maintained by the Archaeological Survey of India as a **heritage** site.*

During the day, locals like to talk to tourists about Kuldhara. But they close the gates to the abandoned village at night—to keep the ghosts inside!

Desolate and Silent

Today, Kuldhara remains abandoned. The deserted village is eerily quiet. The houses look almost identical to the way they looked when the villagers left 200 years ago. It has become a popular tourist destination. Locals often emerge from ruined buildings and tell the village's sad tale to tourists. They may not be ghosts, but they've certainly given a few people a scare!

KOLMANSKOP, AFRICA

Kolmanskop was founded in the early 1900s in the African nation of Namibia. Diamonds were found on top of the sand in the area. As a result, miners traveled to the area to try to find their fortunes. However, the community did not last. It is now totally abandoned. Photos show the village being slowly reclaimed by the desert. Buildings are becoming buried in sand, both inside and out.

Kolmanskop has developed a reputation as a haunted ghost town. This reputation became so widespread that it was investigated by the TV show *Destination Truth*. The show's staff gathered what they considered to be evidence of a haunting. However, paranormal investigation shows like this are often accused of something called confirmation bias. This is when someone takes evidence and forces it to prove what they already believe. So, if someone on a ghost hunting TV show already believes in ghosts, skeptics believe they will turn any evidence into support for their beliefs.

LOOK AT THE EVIDENCE

Today, the reasons for the sudden disappearance of everyone from Kuldhara are still unknown. Maybe the story was true, and a greedy official was to blame. Drought is another possible cause. One recent theory claims that an earthquake made the area impossible to live in. Others believe that trade routes changed, and it was no longer profitable to live in the village. But what about the curse? Is that real? Or did the former residents have another reason for warning people to stay away? Maybe they were hoping to return one day and didn't want anyone to move into their homes. What do you think?

GHOSTS OF THE FORBIDDEN CITY

The Forbidden City in Beijing, China, may be the most impressive palace structure ever built. Made up of 980 buildings, the Forbidden City is a huge, spread-out complex. The royal complex was home to 24 emperors of China over almost 500 years.

In ancient times, it was forbidden to enter or exit the Forbidden City without the emperor's permission.

Bloody History

The Forbidden City has a long and bloody history. Many people have been murdered within its walls. Anyone who went against the emperor's rule was simply removed. The palace was opened to the public in the 1940s. Since then, reports of ghosts and other strange events have become common.

Nighttime is especially spooky. Many report seeing strange monsters, which are said to be the ghosts of animals that guarded the Forbidden City in ancient times. Guards also claim to have seen the ghost of a weeping woman dressed in white. Others say that at midnight, the ghosts of those who were treated badly come out to wander the Forbidden City.

Millions of people visit the complex each year. Some come for the ghost tours!

Woman Without a Face

In China, ghosts are no laughing matter. They're considered dangerous, and people do their best to stay away from them. This is why members of the public are not allowed to enter the Forbidden City after dark. In the 1990s, one guard told a story about a mysterious woman in black. Two of his fellow guards yelled at her, and she ran away from them. Assuming she was a thief, they chased her. Eventually, the guards cornered the woman in front of a locked door. She turned to face the guards, and they almost died of fright. The woman in black had no face!

THE GREAT WALL OF HAUNTING

The Great Wall of China is one of the oldest and most amazing structures ever built by humans. Its earliest parts date back to about 700 B.C.E. The wall was built to protect China from invasion. It stretches over 5,000 miles (8,000 km). Most of the wall was first built between 220 and 226 C.E. During construction, many workers lost their lives. Some estimates put the number of worker deaths at around one million. With that much death around the wall, it's not surprising that some people claim it's haunted. Visitors have seen ghostly figures walking along it. Others say they have heard soldiers marching. Some people have felt sick or suddenly gotten headaches while there.

WHAT DO YOU THINK?

People have told ghost stories for a long time, and they probably always will. As scary as they are, ghost stories can also be comforting. After all, if ghosts are real, then it means some part of us lives on after death. For people who have lost someone, or who worry about dying, these stories can make them feel a little bit better. Many find comfort in thinking that loved ones stay with us and even watch over us after their deaths. There's nothing wrong with that. But some people are all too happy to take advantage of this desire to believe.

Horror films make a lot of money because people love a good scare.

The flickering light and shadows of a campfire make a perfect setting for ghost stories. Some cultures believe that fire is sacred, and that smoke carries messages from the spirit world.

Ghostly Business

There's a long history of people who claim to be able to talk to the dead or see real ghosts. And they're happy to share this with others. Unfortunately, in some cases these people are **swindlers** who are just trying to make money. There's nothing wrong with believing in ghosts. There is something very wrong with misleading people for money.

With that in mind, when you hear a good ghost story, think about it. Why do you think the person is telling it to you? Is it something they really believe happened? Is it just a super-scary story to tell around a campfire? Or are they trying to get something from you?

FAMOUS HOAX OR NOT?

THE AMITYVILLE HORROR

Amityville, New York, is a quiet town with fewer than 10,000 residents. However, it's well-known around the world for a house that's said to be the most haunted in America. The Amityville Horror, as it's known, started in 1974 when the Lutz family bought and moved into the house at 112 Ocean Avenue. Just 28 days later, they fled the place. They claimed they had been pushed out by evil spirits. A very successful book was written about their experiences. The book was then turned into a popular series of horror movies. However, none of the occupants of the house since then has reported supernatural activity.

While there might not have been any ghosts or spirits, there was a real Amityville Horror. Thirteen months before the Lutz family moved in, Ronald DeFeo Jr. murdered his parents and four siblings while they slept. The Lutz family knew about the murders before they bought the house.

Is Amityville really haunted? On the one hand, many skeptics believe the Lutz family invented the story of the hauntings after finding out about the murders. On the other hand, no one has been able to prove that the Amityville ghosts are not real either. The Amityville ghost story is not a proven hoax, just suspected to be. The search for the truth goes on.

LEARNING MORE

BOOKS

Don't Read This Book Before Bed: Thrills, Chills, and Hauntingly True Stories by Anna Claybourne, National Geographic Children's Books, 2017.

Ghost Hunter's Handbook by Liza Gardner Walsh, Down East Books, 2016.

Ghost Towns by Sarah Parvis, National Geographic Learning, 2010.

Handbook to Ghosts, Poltergeists, and Haunted Houses by Sean McCollum, Capstone Press, 2016.

What Was the Underground Railroad? by Yona Zeldis McDonough, Turtleback, reissue edition 2013.

WEBSITES

A site for junior ghost hunters
www.kids.ghostvillage.com/

A list of ghost towns by country
www.wikipedia.org/wiki/List_of_ghost_towns_by_country

Learn more about the Underground Railroad
www.ducksters.com/history/civil_war/underground_railroad.php

Learn more about the L'Anse aux Meadows National Historic Site
http://whc.unesco.org/en/list/4

GLOSSARY

abolitionist A person who supports ending slavery

apparition A ghostly image of a person

archaeologist Someone who studies human history by digging up and studying old objects

boarders People who rent rooms and are provided meals

bootleggers People who made and sold alcohol during Prohibition

critically To think carefully to make an informed judgment about something

electromagnetic field A field of force that has electric and magnetic parts

evidence Facts or information that indicate if something is true or not

Gaelic The traditional language of Scotland and Ireland

gored Stabbed with a horn or tusk of an animal

heritage Considered to be important to a country or area's culture or history

highwaymen Thieves on horseback who robbed travelers at gunpoint

horticulturist A professional who grows fruits, vegetables, flowers, or other plants

night vision Ability to see in the dark

omen A sign of good or evil

orb A sphere, or a three-dimensional circle

paranormal Beyond normal scientific understanding

phenomena Rare or important events, often without a clear cause

Prohibition The law in the United States from 1920 to 1933 that forbade the manufacturing and sale of alcohol

prospector A person who looks for mineral deposits

sanatorium A hospital for people with serious diseases

skeptic A person who doubts the truth of something

schooner A type of sailing ship

specters Ghosts

supernatural Out of the ordinary; not explained by science

swindlers Persons who cheat other people or businesses out of money

tuberculosis An infectious disease of the lungs

Underground Railroad A network of houses and other places used to help slaves from the United States escape to freedom

INDEX